Why we need anti-capitalist resistance

Why we need anti-capitalist resistance

Simon Hannah

Resistance Books

Simon Hannah is a local government worker and a socialist and trade union activist. He is the author of *A Party with Socialists in it: a history of the Labour Left* (2018: Pluto Press), *Can't Pay, Won't Pay: the fight to stop the Poll Tax* (2020: Pluto Press), and *Radical Lambeth 1978-1991* (2021: Breviary Stuff).

In October 1999 the BBC conducted an online poll to decide who was the 'greatest thinker' of the last thousand years.' By a wide margin the winner was Karl Marx, followed by Albert Einstein. This was not a bad feat considering Marx had died in 1883, but it was a testament to the central role the ideas of Marx (and his co-writer Friedrich Engels) played in the court of human history. Marx was an intellectual who believed that capitalism as a system was holding back human potential and had to be replaced with a more radical system – what he called communism. This pamphlet will give an outline of Marxism and how it can help us in the fight to free people and planet from exploitation.

Why we need anti-capitalist resistance

Simon Hannah

Published 2021
Resistance Books, London

ISBN: 978-0-902869-45-5 (print)
ISBN: 978-0-902869-46-2 (e-book)

Cover design Adam di Chiara

CONTENTS

1 │ What is capitalism?   1

2 │ A better world   18

3 │ What is Anti*Capitalist
Resistance   39

4 │ What we stand for   41

What is capitalism?

We live in a capitalist world. And that world is killing us. Capitalism is an economic system where production is privately owned by a small number of people, while the vast majority of us are forced to work for a wage. Our ability to work, our labour power, is a commodity, bought and sold on the market by the boss class. Our labour creates the profit that feeds the capitalist machine. As such, we are exploited wage labourers who are not paid the value of the work we produce. All around us there is 'capital'. Capital is money that makes more money through becoming things: 'commodities'. Capitalism commodifies everything and sells it back to us.

The constant struggle between bosses and workers is a feature of daily life. At the extreme end you have Amazon, with Jeff Bezos, now one of the richest men on the planet, while the logistics workers in Amazon warehouses are badly paid and overworked. Their every movement is tracked. While they are at work their bodies are not their own, they belong to the company. Toilet breaks are frowned on because they cut into work time. A device is strapped to their body, which makes a warning noise if they move too slowly.

In such a place, if you try to organise and join a trade union (even though it is your legal right), then your hours will be cut and you can end up with no shifts. People are sacked to remove trade union organisers from the workplace. Staff are made to watch anti-union 'training videos' about how if you have a problem at work, you should just speak to Human Resources. When you do, they will too often operate to police you as a worker within the company. The message is, 'whatever you do – don't join a union'. Security guards are even hired to keep union organisers from the premises.

Amazon is only an extreme version of what happens to workers all over the world. In factories making Apple products, the work conditions are so bad many workers have committed suicide by throwing themselves from the roof. The company's response? Not to slow down the work schedule or increase pay, but to install nets to prevent people falling to their deaths. During a global pandemic, workers are forced into work to do unnecessary jobs just to keep the profits flowing.

The COVID-19 pandemic shows the brutal reality of the contradictions of the capitalist system, that there is a rupture between people and planet, between our society and the environment, between human health and corporate profit. The drive for profit is killing people while apologists for the system complain about too much 'regulation' and 'health and safety gone mad'.

When you challenge these practices, it is clear that there is no workplace democracy. Every workplace has a strict management hierarchy. Command and control of labour is key to the smooth functioning of capitalism. Capitalism is good at divide and rule. Some start as workers and progress through the management chain, their pay increased because they are being incorporated into the logic of capital. They become the representatives of capital in the workplace. Some workers have more opportunities at work than others; in a country such as Britain, Black workers or women workers have faced prejudice over what roles they can do. Today the wage gap between workers of colour or women workers and white male workers remains considerable.

Why is the world this way? Karl Marx and Friedrich Engels argued that what was going on was class struggle between the bosses and the workers over profit. Profit is created not at the point of selling, but at the point of production. Profit is from not paying workers the full value of your work. Your wages are an agreed reimbursement for your time and energy, your labour power. This is true whether you are a blue-collar manual worker, a white-collar office worker, a university academic, a nurse or in any other waged role. This is why all work is ultimately exploitative; even if you get a pay increase and live a relatively comfortable life as a worker, you are still not being paid the full value of your labour power – if you were, your boss would make no profits.

The difference between your wages and the

value of what you produce is surplus value. And it is this surplus value that is fought over when workers want a shorter working day or higher wages and the bosses want the opposite. When Google creates an HQ with beanbags and pool tables and 'hang out spaces', it is not because they want to make your life more comfortable; it's because they want to keep you in work longer, coding or whatever else it is you are hired to do.

One of the things Marx and Engels wrote about was the idea of 'alienation', that we are cut off from ourselves and exist in a world where things are strangely detached. We are even cut off from our bodies, so we become frightened of our bodies breaking down, frightened they cannot get the work done. Men are separated from women, and women often do not even have control of their own bodies, to choose when to have sex and whether to have children. Our lives are dominated by 'market forces', as if the economy exists beyond us, even though we are a key part of it. We are surrounded by commodities, things that we are told we need to fulfil us. That is not to say that Marxists want a kind of primitive life without modern things, it is that the things we are sold are things that we have made that have been taken from you and then they are sold back to us by the capitalists.

Everyone can relate to how alienating work is under capitalism. A lot of it involves jobs we don't enjoy, which are not socially useful. Jobs people might originally enjoy, end up being exhausting. Because work is controlled by the capitalists, you find a bizarre situation every time there is an economic crisis with the bosses making millions unemployed because they there is 'no more work'.

When 'austerity' is announced by the government, it is always working people who pay. But an economic crisis doesn't change the number of people who need food, clothes, local amenities, education, social work support, transport and so on. This is because the concept of work is captured and distorted by the capitalist system. It is not something natural and joyous as a part of human life and society, it is mercenary and 'economic' in the most alienating sense.

When capitalism took off as an economic system over 200 years ago – quite a short time in human history – women were actively involved as workers. Then women were shunted to the side-lines, into the family to look after children and the men who would go out to work in the factory as the breadwinner. This history of women's work is lost, forgotten, and women are now either treated as objects – even their bodies treated like things to be sold – or exploited in the huge 'service sector' for their 'feminine' abilities, which come from their time in the home looking after the kids and men, and parents, and anyone else who needs care. The service sector, the shops and the entertain-ment and health industries (where people are em-ployed to be nice to other people), is now largely occupied by women. But, notice it is the men who are still often the big managers, and usually the owners, the ones who benefit from women's labour.

This is why resistance by women in organised movements is a crucial part of socialist struggle against capitalism. The nature of social oppression means that self-organisation is an important part of movements against capitalism. Campaigns for equal wages, against sexual violence, the #MeToo movement for example, target the gendered nature of capitalism. Women suffering sexism at work are workers, as are Black people suffering racism and building their own resistance. We might organise separately against our exploitation and oppression, but we strike together against the system.

Some people will tell you that it would be nicer if women were capitalists, or Black people owned companies. When Lehman Brothers collapsed in 2008 some feminists said it would not have happened if it was 'Lehman Sisters'. This is an illusion. There are plenty of illusions that capitalism will peddle to draw people into the system and to divide the working class.

Some try and escape this logic by becoming self-employed or starting their own businesses. They want to escape wage exploitation by being 'their own person' or 'their own boss'. Most of the dreams wither and die within a couple of years – they enter the marketplaces of already established businesses who have market share and struggle to compete. The big boys of capitalism don't play nicely with new rivals. Still, every so often some small enterprise makes a breakthrough (after all, McDonalds used to just be one burger joint in Des

Plaines, Illinois), and the feel-good media machine moves into operation to exalt them – communicating that you too could be rich like this person one day. They are the exceptions to lure you into a belief that capitalism promotes social mobility, that you can be anything you want with hard work and a little luck. These are lies to make the reality of economic life easier to swallow.

Small scale capitalism as a better alternative is an impossible fiction. Capital is driven by accumulation. Capitalists must grow or be overtaken by competitors; capitalism is rapacious and greedy. Money has to make money. Larger companies float on the stock market and require huge lines of credit from banks – the shareholders and financial institutions demand their money; they want a return on investments. Big business has to thrive, reinvent itself, destroy competitors, whatever it takes to keep the profit flowing. Within the chaos of this market economy, people are tossed and dragged through the mud, all at the behest of corporations and capitalist institutions that relentlessly exploit.

Capitalism is a system of exploitation not just

of people, but the planet. It is now clear to anyone (except those in the pay of the petrochemical giants) that global warming and climate change is primarily driven by fossil fuel burning activities. Fossil fuel is the lifeblood of energy production and therefore of capitalist production. It runs through everything. And the oil companies knew in the 1970s that their activities were going to heat the planet to dangerous levels – their response? They didn't just coverup reports, but they also spent millions on propaganda and lies to deny global warming was happening. Tobacco companies did the same around the dangers of smoking. All in the name of profit.

The brutal destruction of the planet in the interests of profit is the clearest example for all to see that capitalism is a system that creates a metabolic rift with nature. Humans live alongside other animals on the planet, we require the planet to sustain ourselves, yet capitalism as a system of mass commodity production driven by profit is destroying the ecosystem. Socialists do not believe in retreating to a more primitive society of subsistence farming, we believe in re-establishing the balance between human society and the natural world through democratically planning our economy and resources.

None of this is to say that the lives of millions have not improved under capitalism. We have seen stunning technological and social changes. The system has gone as far as it can to drag humanity into the modern age. But the cost is too great, the threat to our future too severe, the limitations too rigid; it is time to move beyond capitalism. Capitalism eats at our planet and lives.

We need to take the economy out of the hands of the capitalists. They are a tiny proportion of humanity who enjoy unimaginable wealth with little or no care for workers and the poor. Even so-called 'philanthropists' like Bill Gates, who is spending most of his fortune on health initiatives around the world, only got wealthy through an army of tech engineers, computer programmers and workers on the assembly line making Microsoft products to sell. Without them he would just be a guy in his garage soldering motherboards into PC cases. Now he feels compelled to 'give back' from his vast wealth. We don't celebrate that; we want a world where we don't rely on a handful of billionaires to help vaccinate entire countries. What a ridiculous system to live in. But there are powerful forces maintaining the status quo that need to be fought.

The capitalist state

Capitalism is reinforced and perpetuated by a political and social structure that exists for the benefit of capitalism. The political structure of most capitalist states is to have a parliament that passes laws and an executive wing that enforces those laws (police, prisons, etc). The political structure operates on the basis that capitalism is permanent and natural, that professional politicians are elected every few years to pass laws, while real power exists through the wealth and control of the capitalist class.

The state is not neutral under capitalism, it exists to defend the property, privilege and power of the capitalists. In a society such as Britain, where popular pressure has produced reforms and improvements in workers' lives, there are also laws that are beneficial, but these are only agreed so long as they leave the underlying power structure unchanged. The police and law courts impose the laws that defend the wealthy, and as the old saying goes, property is 9/10ths of the law. That isn't to say that police don't also (occasionally) solve crimes perpetrated against working people or deal with anti-social behaviour, but when a major political crisis comes, they are the first line of defence to protect the established order.

This is a key difference between revolutionaries and reformists. A reformist believes you can get socialism through election to parliament and passing laws that incrementally, gradually, transform capitalism into socialism. Revolutionaries support reforms in parliament that improve lives, but they know that at a certain point the capitalist state will act to prevent radical change. Remember when unnamed generals in the British army warned there would be a 'coup' if Corbyn was elected Prime Minister? When footage was leaked of soldiers using Jeremy Corbyn's face for target practice? There were rumours of coups organised and plotted in the 1970s against the Labour government in case it was too radical.

The reality is that no ruling class has ever given up power peacefully. And the capitalist ruling class is not democratic, they do not abide by the laws. The capitalist class hoard their money abroad and engage in systematic tax avoidance, they threaten to close their businesses if a left-wing government is elected, and some of them fund far right networks. The capitalist class is not going to just surrender peacefully and give up their power and wealth because some socialists won an election.

Yet some socialists believe that there is a parliamentary route to ending capitalism. While politicians like to think that they are powerful, they also realise that ultimately whenever MPs are forced by popular demand to take serious action against the capitalist class, even they have little power. How many times have politicians said they cannot pass various laws because the capitalists will respond with economic sabotage, tanking the stock market, causing a run on the pound and so on?

Class interests can be seen absolutely clearly in the policy decisions that governments make, especially in crisis. When the 2008 financial crash happened there were billions for the big banks to keep finance afloat, but millions of people were forced to use foodbanks to feed their families. The COVID-19 pandemic in 2020 exposed clearly the conflict that exists between the needs of ordinary people struggling with a health crisis and the demands of business. The drive was to keep people in work and businesses open, but many companies going cap-in-hand to receive bailouts from governments sacked their workers anyway.

Global capitalism

Capitalism is not a system that can exist in just one country. It has to spread, penetrate new markets and find new sources of profit. Capitalism as a system of mass commodity production originated in Europe and spread across the world through force of arms, thanks to colonialism. Capitalism transformed human beings into commodities to be bought and sold in the form of chattel slavery – and developed elaborate theories of racism to justify this practice. That is why anti-racist movements have the potential to be a real anti-capitalist force; against the history of racism in the form of colonialism, and the way that racism operates today under capitalism.

As capitalism enriched a handful of western countries, the nature of these economies changed. Some businesses got so big and complex they required more money from banks and other large financial institutions. This led to powerful corporations, a fusion of finance and industrial capital that could ruthlessly expand. The huge increase in revenue and profits enriched the country they were based in – and so states spent huge amounts on military forces that they could deploy to protect their economic interests. These handful of countries projecting that kind of economic and military (and therefore also political) power are imperialist powers. They shaped the world in their interests and used their power to bully smaller and weaker nations to do what they wanted.

As imperialism developed throughout the 19th and 20th centuries, it led to two devastating world wars, as competing imperialist powers struggled for dominance. Since the end of World War Two, European imperialist states have attempted to avoid war by collaborating more closely and integrating their economies – that is the basis of the European Union. The strength of the imperialist nations, and in particular the USA as a global superpower, led to institutions like the World Bank and the International Monetary Fund being established, which have devastated so much of the global south. The United Nations, intended to be a neutral and powerful arbiter of world politics, in practice is toothless, as it cannot realistically act against the interests of the major global powers that created it. The ideals of the UN exist largely on paper.

Appreciating the global nature of the world and the hierarchy of nation states is crucial for Marxists. Imperialism is a brutal form of capitalism that subjugates and destroys billions of people in the interests of a tiny minority. This is why a critical analysis of capitalism means being critical of imperialism too.

A better world

We have talked about the problems of capitalism, but what is the solution? Instead of market capitalism where production, distribution and exchange are in the control of the capitalist class, socialists fight for a democratically planned economy, where producers and consumers make decisions. The aim of socialism is to overthrow the old ruling class and replace it with a society where the majority is the ruling class.

Socialism is ingrained in the way workers fight back under capitalism. Workers know that to resist their bosses they need to be organised. If the capitalists are co-ordinated to act in their class interests, then workers must be too. This realisation transforms a worker into being a part of the working class. We act as a class because we go from atomised individuals to a collective with a shared interest. From this position, the working class can use its industrial strength within production and distribution to place demands on the bosses.

This is why trade unions exist; they are collectives of workers organised as workers. These demands can be small (a modest increase in wages for instance), or significant – when faced with massive redundancies or even the closure of industries, workers might occupy their workplaces, carrying on production under workers' control and demanding that the state intervene to save the failing business. This is why socialists support strikes and industrial action by workers – they pose the possibility of a different way or organising the economy, they challenge the logic of exploitation and capital, and reveal how crucial workers are to the economy.

The struggle of workers against their exploitation lays the basis of socialism. A reactionary minister in Europe warned many years ago that 'behind every strike lurks the hydra of revolution' – those with established power know that working class resistance is powerful, that it threatens the existing order. That is why so much energy and time is spent convincing workers to be passive, to be obedient, not to question authority, and to shift the blame onto people from other countries or who hold different religions.

A socialist state is not like a capitalist one with a privileged tiny clique of powerful people making all the decisions; it is based on mass popular democracy. That is why the creation of committees of struggle, workplace occupations, or assemblies is such an important part of the class war. These create in embryo the forums that could build a revolutionary state. The goal is a classless and stateless society, where we can live as equals, where old divisions along lines of gender, nationalism or ethnicity are pointless and forgotten.

A true liberation of humanity from the oppression of class society and exploitation. Socialism will end meaningless and crap jobs and replace them with meaningful work. It is a system that can rationally plan the economy so that work is distributed fairly, which will lead to reducing the working week. Ending capitalism means that the surplus value from someone's work is no longer stolen by the capitalists, which means that wages can rise dramatically.

Such a system will also radically reset our relationship to the planet. We do not need to cut down the Amazon rainforest for logging or farming. We can distribute the food we already have – half of the food we produce is wasted, most dumped in the ocean or in landfill sites. That kind of irrational waste will end. We can also move away from fossil fuel energy production in a planned and rapid way, without having to worry about what shareholders and directors of major corporations think.

Socialist politics

This principle of striving for working class unity is why socialists are opposed to divisions along the lines of gender, race and nationality. Workers have more in common with each other, regardless of religion, ethnicity or language. It is a tragic weakness of workers today that so many identify with their rich bosses and politicians, just because they speak the same language and have the same passport, than with their working class siblings across the world.

This is one of the reasons the left defends migrants against the right-wing narrative that they are 'flooding our country' or that they are somehow taking jobs or changing our culture. Working class culture is always changing, it is very different now than it was 200 years ago when children were sent up chimneys and most of us couldn't read. We reject the view that culture is static and unchanging. Likewise, we reject the idea that migrant workers are the enemy, that they are the cause of problems in society – the problems come from the top, not from below. As the saying goes "The enemy doesn't arrive by boat. He arrives by limousine."

This is why socialists also oppose wars, like the Iraq war. Wars are fought in the interests of capitalists to carve up the world and its resources. They send soldiers – most recruited from the working class – into battle as cannon fodder to secure economic and political advantages. Socialists oppose such wars and argue against the reasons why they are fought, exposing the lies that the wars are fought for 'freedom' when it is clear as day that there are always ulterior motives.

And whilst socialists focus on the working class because the working class has the power to end capitalism and change the world for the better, they also take seriously the fight for national and social liberation. In some parts of the world whole peoples are oppressed and denied their national rights, like the Palestinians, Kurds, the Catholics in Northern Ireland, the Tamils in Sri Lanka and so on. Socialists support the struggles of those people for their national rights. The struggles of women, LGBTQ people, disabled and racialised people for equality are also central to progressive left politics. Socialists hold no illusions that capitalism will ever allow for genuine equality between people or between nations.

Marxism provides the tools to understand the way the world works and what motivates political and economic actions. It means we can examine the world without falling into conspiracy theories. Behind an action like the Iraq war there is an agenda, yes, but it is structured into the system, not because there are bizarre hidden conspiracies by Freemasons or Jews or Lizard-people or aliens. Being consciously and collectively organised is the opposite of falling for stupid conspiracy theories. Those conspiracy theories make us powerless and divide us from each other. Think, mobilise, act together, each of us respecting each other.

Counter-revolution

The ruling class does not sit back and just allow rebellion from below. To defend capitalism there is soft and hard power that act to undermine resistance, sow division and defeat the left. This includes racism, sexism and anti-LGBTQ politics that try to divide workers against each other. Capitalism forces competition for jobs, white workers blaming Black or foreign workers for 'taking their jobs' or 'driving down wages' when it is the bosses that make these decisions and play the game of divide and rule. Reactionary ideas of women not being as good as men, or being limited to domestic roles are still common, even after decades of women fighting for equality. Homophobia is now frowned upon officially, but arch reactionaries still put the heterosexual nuclear family on a pedestal, lambasting LGBTQ people for being different or 'odd' compared to others. Transphobia is rife across society.

The media acts to 'manufacture consent', as Noam Chomsky describes, to bolster the dominant ideology of the capitalist system. This isn't because journalists are part of a conspiracy, but because the mainstream media reflects the dominant values of the society in which it operates. This means that the spectrum of the press in Britain is a narrow one between Conservative and Liberal. It is the same with judges; they come from the ranks of the middle and upper classes, are schooled in bourgeois law and reflect the values of the society in which that law operates. It is important not to see capitalism as just a conspiracy of a tiny minority, it is all around us and needs to be challenged ideologically as well as politically.

At the extreme end of politics there are far right, fascistic movements and parties that advocate for white supremacy and are actively violent against the left (who they see as traitors) and anyone different from them. Fascism took power in

Italy and Germany and Spain before World War Two to prevent socialist revolution from happening, slaughtering thousands before 1939 and then millions during the war in a bizarre death cult that hated communists, Jews and the disabled (among many others) and tried to create nation states rooted in violence.

Right-wing populists and Fascists use lies and demagogy to whip up hatred against progressive ideas and movements. They represent despair and a desire to return to a mythical past of a 'great country' that never existed. In this way they are on the same end of the spectrum as Conservative parties, but those parties have a far more mainstream outlook, operating (generally) within the rules of the state and government. Fascists are willing to opportunistically use political structures to get more prominence and power, but they are also violent counter-revolutionaries who, if given the opportunity, will destroy democracy.

This was the danger with Brexit and people like Donald Trump. Desperate people look for simple solutions – blame foreigners, blame Muslims, demand 'national independence' (whatever that means for a powerful already sovereign nation). But these are false solutions – worse than that, they can be dangerous. Nationalism in an imperialist country like Britain or the USA will always unleash reactionary views among the wider population, a sense that 'our people' are somehow superior to others, that the soul of the country is eroded by migrants or other countries. It is a demand to make Britain or the USA 'great again', but these are nations built on blood, imperialism, on inflicting famine and poverty across the world to enrich our own. Working class solidarity has to come first, always, and this means across borders. Nationalism in a powerful imperialist country is a sickness that infects working people and binds them to their rulers, all because they speak the same language and have the same passport.

The labour movement

In Britain there is the Labour Party and the trade unions, both of which are organisations that ostensibly fight for working class interests. Trade Unions have been around for as long as capitalism. For many years trade unions were banned by pro-capitalist politicians to stop workers organising and resisting a rapacious capitalism that was making them work 16-hour days. Labour was founded as the Labour Representation Committee in 1900 after some of the trade unions decided that they needed a party in parliament to represent their interests.

But things are not so simple. Trade Unions are important organisations of working-class defensive struggles; workers join them to get higher wages or improve their working conditions. However, as they developed trade unions began to be run by a layer of officials who were often well paid. These officials became a separate bureaucratic caste within the unions, seeing themselves as mediators between the demands of the workers and the bosses. These officials would advocate for their members' demands, but they were not revolutionaries who wanted to get rid of capitalism. While they would talk of socialism, in practice they wanted to reform capitalism to make it more palatable and bearable.

When Labour was formed by the trade union

officials in 1900, it was founded on the same logic – not to replace capitalism or pursue the class struggle, but to get 'sensible' MPs elected to pass laws to improve the position of workers and the poor. It is good that such laws are passed, but this consolidated Labour not as an anti-capitalist party to radically change the system, but as one of gradual reforms. Because Labour is an electoral party that only focuses on parliamentary and council elections, it has on occasion issued quite radical statements when the workers movement is very militant and confident to get votes. But usually, Labour's politics are painfully moderate and it refuses to truly organise people to fight back against capitalism. It just wants their votes every few years. While Labour will wave the red flag and talk about socialism (sometimes), it has never been a party that had any intention of realising socialism.

The history of the Labour Party and trade unions is in many ways one of squandered opportunities and setbacks. Many important gains have been won (the weekend, sick pay, 8 hour working day, the NHS, unemployment benefits, and so on), but these demands came from workers and not the well-paid officials running the movement. There have also been important struggles of workers that Labour politicians or trade union leaders undermined and demobilised; the general strike in 1926 was called off by the trade union leaders even though it was growing in strength; Labour Prime Minister Clement Attlee sent in the army to break strikes by transport workers and dockers after 1945; the Trade Union Congress refused to call a general strike to support the miners in 1984/5; the list goes on.

Despite these criticisms, Socialists understand that we are usually in a minority in most movements and countries. That is why we cannot be sectarian regarding mass movements and organisations. Being a trade unionist in a workplace and organising your workmates is the simplest and often most important thing a socialist can do. It is embryonic and the most basic form of class consciousness to be in a trade union – a starting point for real emancipation. Likewise, when there is a Conservative government, millions will look to Labour as better alternative and believe the rhetoric that Labour stands up for working people.

It isn't enough to denounce the setbacks and betrayals by the official leadership of the movement, it is important to work alongside and with workers, not shying from criticism but proving in action that socialist politics and ways of organising work. We don't need to fight forever in an unending struggle with the capitalist; why don't we build a world where they are no longer in power?

Criticisms

Some claim Marxism is a too simplistic an analysis of society. They argue that the division between workers and capitalists doesn't take into account the complexity of modern economies. But this is a weak criticism because Marxism doesn't analyse society simply in terms of those two antagonistic classes, even though they are essential for capitalism to function. There are also peasants in many countries who own a small piece of land, there are self-employed people and small businesses, in some places there is a large public sector where people are not employed to make profit, but to provide services like education, healthcare and social work.

The nature of work has changed as well. In the early 19th century, when capitalism was first developing in Britain, most workers were rural labourers or textile weavers working with handlooms. When the textile industry declined it was replaced by other industries, including manufacturing and coal mining. In the 20th century, there was a huge explosion of retail, banking and finance and the car industry. Socialists see a direct line between a handloom weaver in Manchester in 1830 and a Deliveroo rider today. They are exploited workers who have to sell their labour power. Yes, the bosses have changed, the industry has changed, the nature of the work has changed, but the *relationship* between boss and worker remains the same.

There are also jobs that used to be thoroughly middle-class professions such as teaching or the civil service, which have been converted into more working-class vocations over the years as the public sector grew. Teachers and civil servants now join trade unions and go on strikes over pay, pensions, and working conditions.

The view that the working class in Britain doesn't exist anymore is also false. It has evolved, changed and shifted, but the working class exists. The main problem for workers today is that a lot of younger workers do not realise their position in society, they do not realise the power of their position as workers. This is in large part due to the decline of trade unionism and socialism in Britain as a mass ideology.

What about the countries that called themselves socialist or even communist like the USSR or East Germany? These were the product of the Russian revolution of 1917 where an alliance of workers, soldiers and peasants led by the Bolsheviks overthrew the government and declared a new one built on popular committees instead of a parliament. But despite their efforts, the revolution did not spread, and failed revolutions in Germany and Hungary left the new socialist country isolated. An invasion of several hostile capitalist countries decimated the economy and caused widespread social crisis. The revolutionary state of the USSR survived, just, but the price of survival was the growth of an increasingly conservative bureaucracy that turned on the revolution, executed many socialists and imposed a police state, known now for its leader, Josef Stalin – Stalinism.

Russia used five-year plans to force industrialisation, but in a brutal fashion. The workers and peasants had no power even though they lived in a country that claimed to be ruled on their behalf. While there was a significant amount of planning of the economy, this was a command economy, ruled from above by a clique. That is not the same as a radical democracy where workers – the majority of the population – make the decisions. When there were pro-democracy movements demanding freedom from the secret police and for votes, the regimes responded with repression, as they did in Hungary in 1956. This is where the term 'tankie' derives; to describe the people on the left who supported the crushing of those workers resisting the dictatorship. Tanks were also used against pro-democracy protestors in Tiananmen square in 1989.

The economies of the so-called socialist states ended up being less and less productive until stagnation set in during the 1970s. It was only a short time until the system went into crisis and mass

popular protests erupted in the 1980s, which overthrew those old regimes. Pro-capitalist forces
emerged, funded by western interests and the
Catholic Church, which built up political parties
advocating integrating those countries into western capitalism. The idea of socialism was tarnished
by the nature of the regimes, which left power in
the hands of the capitalists.

It is easy to look at what happened in those
'socialist' countries and say that socialism was a
failed experiment that should never be tried again.
But socialism is not a single thing or regime – it
is the struggle of workers to take power against
their oppressors. It is inevitable that there will be
failed attempts and setbacks before capitalism is
overthrown. The crucial point now is not to build
a left that glazes over these historical problems or,
worse, argues some revisionist history that the dic-
tatorships weren't that bad, or even represent posi-
tive examples we should strive for today. A left that
is built on such a basis would replicate the same violent and brutal methods.

A criticism of the socialist left today is that
many workers are not socialists, and some of them

even hold arch-reactionary right-wing ideas. This is a crucial point. Workers do not spontaneously and automatically develop a socialist consciousness. The entire capitalist system is weighted towards preventing the formation of socialist ideas among workers. It isn't just the mainstream media pumping out propaganda on a daily basis, it is the widespread ideology of capitalism, which depicts the system as normal and natural. That is why an aggrieved worker might join a trade union and take industrial action to fight for improvements in working conditions, but not draw the conclusion that the system should be overthrown. That is why socialist organisation is so important, because it helps link practice and theory, to explain what the class struggle is and how workers can organise not just to challenge the capitalists, but to overthrow them and liberate themselves.

Anti*Capitalist Resistance

Faced with these challenges we need to get organised. It isn't enough to shout at the TV or shake our heads at the newspaper headlines – we have to fight back. We have to get to the root of the problem: the class power that rules the world and the capitalist system that oppresses us. We have to take seriously struggles for human emancipation, for democracy, for us to live in harmony with the planet. But we know that all reforms, all progress can be challenged and reversed so long as capitalism structures our society.

The left has been through many ups and downs recently. We are under no illusion, the defeat of Corbynism and the continued election of Tory governments has demoralised many people. But we cannot afford to be demoralised, not with climate catastrophe bearing down on us all.

Anti*Capitalist Resistance is a revolutionary socialist organisation. We are attempting to organise a little differently. We are painfully aware of the left's tendency to split and looking at the enormity of our tasks we do not think that a load of tiny sects is going to make enough impact on the class war that the bosses are waging against workers and the devastation being done to the planet. We are attempting to unite wider layers of the left on some basic principles. If you agree with what you have read in this pamphlet, consider joining or coming along to one of our meetings to learn more.

We are ambitious in our desire to make socialism a mass force, to build an organisation that can make a serious difference. We are not saying it will be easy, and there are a lot of lessons still to learn, but we have to try. There is too much at stake. We have a world, *our* world, to win.

3

What is Anti*Capitalist Resistance

We are an organisation of revolutionary socialists. We believe red-green revolution is necessary to meet the compound crisis of humanity and the planet.

We are internationalists, ecosocialists, and anticapitalist revolutionaries. We oppose imperialism, nationalism, and militarism, and all forms of discrimination, oppression, and bigotry. We support the self-organisation of women, Black people, disabled people, and LGBTQI+ people. We support all oppressed people fighting imperialism and forms of apartheid, and struggling for self-determination, including the people of Palestine.

We favour mass resistance to neoliberal capitalism. We work inside existing mass organisations, but we believe grassroots struggle to be the core of effective resistance, and that the emancipation of the working class and the oppressed will be the act of the working class and the oppressed ourselves.

We reject forms of left organisation that focus exclusively on electoralism and social-democratic reforms. We also oppose top-down 'democratic-centralist' models. We favour a pluralist organisation that can learn from struggles at home and across the world.

We aim to build a united organisation, rooted in the struggles of the working class and the oppressed, and committed to debate, initiative, and self-activity. We are for social transformation, based on mass participatory democracy.

info@anticapitalistresistance.org
www.anticapitalistresistance.org

4

What we stand for

The world is facing unprecedented interrelated crises with the coronavirus pandemic, the accelerating climate disaster, creeping fascism, and an economic crash.

Extreme inequality is out of control. There are more billionaires than ever before. Meanwhile, the world's poorest get even poorer as governments bail out private corporations and cut back on education and health. This is no accident, or just the result of greed. It is built into the logic of capitalism, a system built on profit and exploitation of people and planet.

Change is urgent. We need mass movement to win victories for democracy and social, climate and economic justice. We must organise for action now, but also for system change.

Ecosocialism

Anti*Capitalist Resistance calls itself ecosocialist because the ecological crisis is so profound that it redefines the socialist project. We are engaged not just in a struggle to end capitalism and for a socialist society, but also to have a viable planet.

We challenge the growth-based and consumption-driven system of capitalism, which is also responsible for the development of pandemics such as COVID-19. This task is urgent. That's why we need mass movements today that force governments to stop the rise in global warming below 1.5°C by 2030 to prevent catastrophic and irreversible climate change.

Internationalism

Anti-Capitalist Resistance is internationalist and opposes imperialism, nationalism and militarism.

Capitalism is an international system, so the struggle for socialism must be international, uniting workers of all countries. Huge corporations, some bigger than many countries, dominate the world economy. We need to organise across borders for action and solidarity. Socialists oppose imperialism – the subjugation of weaker nations by stronger ones – and support the self-determination of oppressed nations and the struggle for national liberation.

Anti-Capitalist Resistance supports the right of people to challenge colonialism and forms of apartheid and to struggle for self-determination, including for the people of Palestine. We will support a united Ireland and Scotland's right to self-determination, up to and including independence.

Liberation for the oppressed

Capitalism divides working class people along sexual, gendered, racial, national and other distinctions; the oppressed suffer most. The most effective way to fight back is for those who directly experience discrimination to organise and lead their own struggles. Much has been achieved but not liberation. There can be no liberation without socialism, and no socialism without liberation of the oppressed.

Socialists support feminists in their fight for reproductive rights, for equal pay, against patriarchy, and for LGBTQ+ rights. We stand in solidarity with trans* people currently experiencing the sharp end of a backlash against their right to exist and to unconditionally self-define their gender.

We are against racism from the state and in any other form, against immigration controls and borders, and support the struggle for migrant rights. We fight to remove the legacy of slavery and colonialism. We are for the creation of a society without the barriers that exclude those with mental or physical impairments.

The labour movement and socialists must champion these liberation struggles as our own, while recognising the right of the oppressed to lead these struggles and formulate their own demands.

Stop Tories
For a Labour government

The European Union is a neoliberal capitalist trade bloc, but the vote for Brexit has accelerated the shift to the right in politics. We now have a government in the hands of English nationalists, an even more hostile environment for migrants, deepening racism and creeping authoritarianism. The left must now work together to stop the consequences of the Tory Brexit.

Anti-Capitalist Resistance defends in the Labour Party and in the trade unions the political gains won while Jeremy Corbyn was leader of the party. Radical policies against austerity and neoliberalism are popular. That's why Jeremy Corbyn and Bernie Sanders have so many enthusiastic supporters and came under unprecedented attack.

The election of a Labour government at Westminster would be a blow to the hard-right Tory party and would give confidence to millions to fight for deeper change. But the ruling class will only give up their power and wealth through mass struggles of the working class and the oppressed.

That's why Anti*Capitalist Resistance is committed to social change through mass struggle of the working class without focussing exclusively on elections and parliamentary reforms.

We take the culture war seriously as a site of conflict between socialists and reactionaries. As Marxists, we believe that cultural battles are not secondary to economic ones. We oppose the right's distortion of class that defines it as a static, often reactionary identity and reassert Marx's formulation of class as a living process of struggle necessarily involving the mass agency of workers in transforming the world and thereby themselves.

Socialism

Poverty, exploitation, oppression and war are products of the capitalist system in which a tiny minority ruling class benefits from the labour of the majority. The alternative is socialism, where the wealth created is owned in common, major assets such as industry and finance are socialised and democratic planning to meet society's needs.

Socialism is not possible without the fullest possible democracy. It must guarantee freedom of expression and organisation to every range of opinion, other than those who incite violence against the oppressed or the working class.

Anti*Capitalist Resistance is a pluralist and internationalist organisation that can learn from struggles across the world. We are democratic revolutionary socialists and oppose the top-down model of 'democratic-centralist' organisation.

Anti*Capitalist Resistance will encourage convergence with other revolutionary Marxist activists and organisations. Anti*Capitalist Resistance aims to be rooted in the struggles of the working class and the oppressed and is committed to debate, initiative, and self-activity.

Anti*Capitalist Resistance draws its politics from Marxism. The class struggle is still very real. The social crisis caused by COVID has demonstrated that, as workers are sent into workplaces and nurses get sick through the government prioritising capitalism above people. We have a vision of a new society, one based on human freedom, as described in the Communist Manifesto: 'In place of the old bourgeois society, with its classes and class antagonisms, we shall have an association, in which the free development of each is the condition for the free development of all.'

Resolution carried at the Anti*Capitalist Resistance conference 31 January 2021.

ABOUT THE PUBLISHER

RESISTANCE BOOKS is a radical publisher of internationalist, ecosocialist and feminist books. Resistance Books publishes books in collaboration with the International Institute for Research and Education (www.iire.org), and the Fourth International (www.fourth.international/en). For further information, including a full list of titles available and how to order them, go to the Resistance Books website.

info@resistancebooks.org
www.resistancebooks.org